In a While, Crocodile

In a While, Crocodile

New Orleans Slow Cooker Recipes

Patrice Keller Kononchek
Lauren Malone Keller

Photographs by Michael Palumbo

PELICAN PUBLISHING COMPANY
GRETNA 2014

To NOLA's next generation of foodies:
Meredith, Marianne, Christian, and Robert

First printing, January 2014
Second printing, September 2014

The word "Pelican" and the depiction of a pelican are
trademarks of Pelican Publishing Company, Inc., and are
registered in the U.S. Patent and Trademark Office.

Library of Congress Cataloging-in-Publication Data

Kononchek, Patrice Keller.
 In a while, crocodile : New Orleans slow cooker recipes / by Patrice Keller Kononchek and Lauren Malone Keller ; photographs by Michael Palumbo.
    pages cm
 Includes index.
 ISBN 978-1-4556-1842-2 (pbk. : alk. paper) — ISBN 978-1-4556-1843-9 (e-book)
 1. Electric cooking, Slow. 2. Cooking, American—Louisiana style. I. Keller, Lauren Malone. II. Title.
 TX827.K65 2014
 641.5'884—dc23

                                                            2013024515

Printed in Malaysia
Published by Pelican Publishing Company, Inc.
1000 Burmaster Street, Gretna, Louisiana 70053

Contents

Preface

Here in New Orleans, we don't eat to live—we live to eat! With more than one thousand fabulous restaurants in our great city, we are fortunate to have so many hidden local gems to discover and so many old favorites to frequent.

Born and raised in New Orleans, we have fond early memories of evenings spent with family at various New Orleans restaurants. Later, when we graduated from college and became young professionals with a (little) disposable income, we found ourselves dining out as often as possible. We embraced our local cuisine with reckless abandon.

Alas, with time came responsibility. Year by year, expenses grew and free time faded. We went from being young, carefree professionals to being home-owning professionals with children and with husbands attending evening graduate-school programs. It was time for us to stare reality in the face—it was time for us to learn how to cook!

Accepting our fate with trepidation, we began by collecting family recipes and recipes from our favorite restaurants. As sisters-in-law, it was practical to pool our resources. We resolved that if we couldn't dine out, at least we would do our best to recreate those delectable meals in our own homes. We worked hard, and we learned a lot. Unfortunately, many of our favorite meals were very time-consuming and required us to be tied to the stove for an impossible number of minutes. We thought long and hard until, finally, a light bulb went off. What if we used the most overlooked appliance every newlywed is gifted: the slow cooker?

So began our journey. Through much trial and error, we managed to compile a go-to arsenal of easy, low-maintenance adaptations of cherished New Orleans recipes . . . with a little lagniappe, of course! So bust out your slow cooker and fire it up. Your favorite New Orleans meals will be ready in a while, crocodile!

Bon Appétit!

Acknowledgments

Together, we would like to thank all of the wonderful people who contributed their time, talent, and effort to the making of this book.

We would like to thank Bobby Keller for sharing his gift of cooking brilliance and Sue Keller for sharing her creative ideas and unparalleled love and support.

We are thankful to the delightful Fred and Kathy Kononchek for contributing a few of their top-notch recipes—their gumbo is simply amazing.

We thank photographer Michael Palumbo for being as excited as we are about this book and for his painstaking attention to detail, which has made these photographs sing.

We thank Pelican Publishing Company for this opportunity and for the liberty to be creative throughout this process to bring our vision to life.

Patrice would also like to thank Aunt Kathie for being such a dear friend. She would especially like to thank her husband, the love of her life, Chris. For ten years, he has supported all of her crazy ventures with patience, humor, and enthusiasm. This book would not be possible without him.

Lauren would like to thank her support network: her sisters, Alison and Kristin, and the Malone, Greenleaf, Thomas, and Jaynes families. She is grateful to her parents and to the friends who have become family. She would especially like to thank Rob, her witty, loving, selfless best friend and husband. He inspires us all to squeeze every drop out of every day we're given.

Above all, we would like to thank God, from whom all good things come and through whom all things are possible.

In a While, Crocodile

Appetizers

Bucktown Barbecue Shrimp

Whenever we have a hankering for fresh seafood, we head to Bucktown, the local hub of mom-and-pop seafood shops.

We stock up on fresh jumbo shrimp to make this meal, inspired by one of our favorite restaurants, Pascal's Manale. Barbecue shrimp is the embodiment of New Orleans cuisine: butter, fresh seafood, and spices—a little messy, a little slow, but absolutely satisfying.

Don't forget the essential sidekicks for this dish: a bib, napkins, and lots of French bread to soak up the sauce! *Serves 4-6*

1 cup butter
2 cloves garlic, minced
1¼ cups Worcestershire sauce
3 tbsp. lemon juice
2 tsp. olive oil

2 tbsp. black pepper
2 tbsp. paprika
2 tsp. hot sauce
2-3 lbs. fresh head-on jumbo
   shrimp

Add all ingredients except for the shrimp to the slow cooker and stir.

Cook on high heat for 2 to 2½ hours.

Add shrimp to sauce and stir to coat.

Cook for 1 hour or until shrimp are pink and opaque but not rubbery.

Note: Once you add the shrimp, it is important to monitor them and stir occasionally, as cooking times will vary with different slow cookers. You want the shrimp to be bright, pink, and opaque when you remove them from the heat.

Satchmo Shrimp Dip

"Do you know what it means to miss New Orleans?"

If the essence of New Orleans could be captured by one voice, it would be that of Louis Armstrong. Raspy, soulful, and emoting true joie de vivre, Satchmo's singing exemplifies the spirit of the Big Easy.

This no-fuss dip is perfect for a laid-back New Orleans evening of good food, good music, and good company. *Serves 6-8*

½ cup mayonnaise
½ cup sour cream
1 8-oz. block cream cheese, softened
¼ cup butter
1 cup parmesan cheese, shredded
1 cup mozzarella cheese, shredded

5 green onions, chopped
1 clove garlic, minced
1 lb. fresh shrimp, peeled and deveined
3-4 slices cooked bacon, crumbled, for garnish

Add all ingredients except for the bacon to the slow cooker and stir.

Cook on low heat for 1½ to 2 hours.

Top with crumbled bacon.

Creole Crab Dip

We love our seafood here in New Orleans. In fact, we prefer our calendar year divided into seafood seasons instead of months: crawfish season, oyster season, redfish season, crab season . . .

During crab season—generally the warmest months—this warm and savory dip is a real treat. Slice baguettes diagonally into thin slices, toast, and spread the crab dip to make a bruschetta-like finger food. Melba toast rounds or fancy crackers are also great companions for this dip. *Serves 8-10*

8 oz. cream cheese, softened
½ large onion, diced
8 oz. fresh crab meat
½ cup mayonnaise

1 tsp. prepared horseradish
2 tbsp. lemon juice
1 tbsp. Creole seasoning
1 tsp. hot sauce

Combine all ingredients in the slow cooker.

Cook on low heat for 2 hours, stirring occasionally.

Serve with toast, crackers, or sliced veggies.

Note: If you like more kick, double the horseradish!

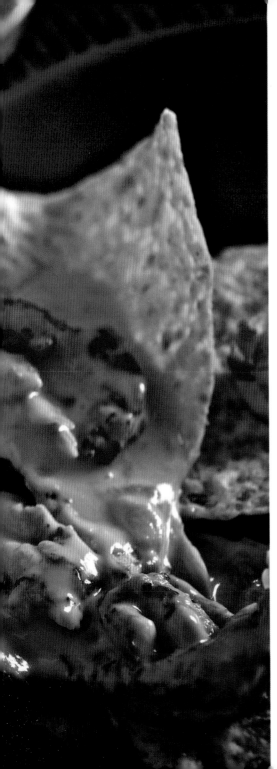

Cajun Queso

For a quick and simple appetizer to bring to a party, this is our go-to recipe. The down-home seasoning adds just enough spice to give it kick but not so much that it scares anyone off.

On more than one occasion, we've caught guests adding a few dollops to their dinner plate as an extra topping for their meal. We suppose that you can't go wrong adding this creamy, zesty, delicious dip to any dish! *Serves 4-6*

½ lb. white American cheese
4 oz. heavy whipping cream
1 4-oz. can green chilies
¾ tsp. Creole seasoning, plus
  additional to taste

½ lb. crawfish tails, cooked
Tortilla chips, for serving

Grease the slow cooker.

In the slow cooker, combine all ingredients except for the crawfish tails and chips.

Cook on high heat for 1 to 1½ hours, stirring occasionally.

Add crawfish tails 20 to 30 minutes before serving.

Once heated through, serve with tortilla chips.

Steamboat Stuffed Artichokes

These artichokes are the perfect pairing for any number of meals. They steam well in the slow cooker, making the leaves very tender. We particularly enjoy them as an opening act for Italian meals. During crawfish season, we like to nibble on them while the mudbugs are cooking! *Serves 6-8*

3 large artichokes
1 cup grated Romano cheese
1 cup Italian breadcrumbs
1 clove garlic, minced
½ tsp. salt
½ tsp. pepper

Olive oil
Lemon slices, for garnish
Paprika, for garnish
Feta cheese, optional, for garnish

Wash artichokes and trim the stems and tops of leaves.

In a large bowl, combine Romano cheese, breadcrumbs, garlic, salt, and pepper.

Using your fingers, push mixture between the artichoke leaves.

Place artichokes in the slow cooker and drizzle olive oil over them. Add enough water to cover the bottom third of the artichokes.

Cook on high heat for 3 to 4 hours or until leaves are tender.

Remove artichokes with tongs. Place a lemon slice on top of each artichoke and sprinkle with paprika. Top with feta, if desired.

Lagniappe Spinach and Artichoke Dip

We New Orleanians love our lagniappe—that little unexpected something extra. While this dip is similar to many traditional spinach and artichoke dip recipes, we kicked it up with some good ol' fashioned Louisiana lagniappe. The hot sauce and Creole seasoning add depth and heat. Feel free to tone it down or add more to suit your taste. *Serves 8-10*

2 8-oz. blocks cream cheese
1 8-oz. block mozzarella cheese
1 8-oz. block Monterey cheese
1 14-oz. can artichoke hearts, drained and chopped
1 14-oz. bag frozen spinach, thawed and drained
5 cloves garlic, minced
¼ tsp. ground black pepper, or to taste
¼ tsp. Creole seasoning, or to taste
1 tsp. hot sauce, or to taste

Cut blocks of mozzarella, Monterey, and cream cheese into 1" cubes.

Add all ingredients to the slow cooker and stir.

Cook on high heat for 1 to 2 hours or until fully melted, stirring occasionally.

Marigny Mushrooms

The Faubourg Marigny neighborhood is a hidden treasure for us locals. We love the architectural details of the brightly painted old homes and the fun, eccentric vibe of the many artists, musicians, and free spirits who live in the area.

Like the Marigny, these mushrooms are bold, lively, and full of flavor! Serve them with toothpicks at a party, or, if you want to get fancy, serve them on top of a juicy steak and use the sauce as gravy for mashed potatoes. *Serves 6-8*

4 cups whole button
   mushrooms
½ cup butter
1 cup sugar

1¼ cups soy sauce
1½ cups water
½ tsp. garlic salt

Clean mushrooms and remove their stems.

Place mushrooms in the slow cooker.

Cover mushrooms with remaining ingredients and stir.

Cook on low heat for 8 hours.

Mardi Gras Meatballs

Aside from the ornate floats, the festive throws, and the sounds of marching bands reverberating through the streets, one of our favorite things about Mardi Gras is simply the opportunity to be social. During Carnival season, we like to head over to the homes of friends who live on the parade route.

These meatballs are our favorite recipe for Mardi Gras parties, and they're always a hit! Simple to make, these are sweet with a little kick. Keep them hot by bringing them to the party in the slow cooker and using the "warm" setting. *Serves 10-12*

1 64-oz. bag frozen, prepared, pre-cooked meatballs
1 27-oz. jar grape jelly

1 12-oz. bottle chili sauce
2 tbsp. brown sugar
½ tsp. Worcestershire sauce

Place meatballs and all remaining ingredients in the slow cooker. Stir to combine and coat meatballs thoroughly.

Cook on low heat for 3 to 4 hours or until juices from the meatballs run clear.

Serve with toothpicks.

Soups and Stews

Treme (Mock) Turtle Soup

When it comes to cooking, we like things to be quick and easy—as long as flavor is not sacrificed. However, when it comes to soup, we realize that an extra few minutes of prep work make a real difference in the richness and quality of a recipe.

Quickly sautéing vegetables before adding them to the slow cooker scales back their acidity and firmness. Allowing them to then simmer in the slow cooker for hours allows all of the ingredients to meld. It's the perfect formula for a successful soup! *Serves 4-6*

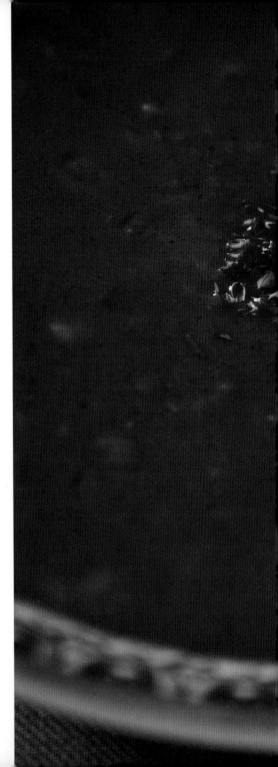

1½ lbs. ground sirloin
6 stalks celery, chopped
2 cloves garlic, minced
1 cup chopped onion
¾ cup butter
1 15-oz. can tomato puree
2 14.5-oz. cans chicken broth
2 14.5-oz. cans beef broth
½ cup flour mixed with 1 cup
    water
½ cup Worcestershire sauce

1 cup ketchup
1 tsp. hot sauce
2 bay leaves
1½ tsp. thyme
Salt and pepper to taste
½ cup lemon juice
¼ cup flat-leaf parsley, minced
6 hard-boiled eggs, chopped
6 slices lemon, for garnish
1 cup sherry, or to taste,
    optional

On the stovetop, sauté the sirloin, celery, garlic, and onion in butter until meat is brown and veggies are translucent. Add to the slow cooker.

Add tomato puree, chicken broth, beef broth, flour mixture, Worcestershire sauce, ketchup, hot sauce, bay leaves, thyme, salt, and pepper to the slow cooker. Stir.

Cook on low heat for 4 hours.

Add lemon juice, parsley, and eggs 30 minutes before serving.

Immediately before serving, remove bay leaves, add sherry to taste, and garnish with lemon slices.

Chartres Cajun White Bean and Sausage Soup

A little less populated by tourists than its neighboring streets of Bourbon and Royal, Chartres Street affords all the charm of the Quarter. Its wrought-iron balconies showcase colorful ferns, flowers, and flags, while the street below houses art galleries, funky boutiques, and restaurants galore.

This hearty, savory soup will call to mind the classic spirit of a French Quarter café. *Serves 4-6*

1 lb. andouille or smoked sausage, sliced into ½" rounds
1 lb. dried navy beans, rinsed
2 carrots, halved lengthwise and sliced
3 stalks celery, chopped
1 large yellow onion, chopped
¼ tsp. pepper
½ tsp. cumin
¼ tsp. red pepper flakes
1 bay leaf
4 14.5-oz. cans chicken broth
¼ cup chopped fresh parsley
Cooked bacon, crumbled, for garnish
Chopped green onions, for garnish

In the slow cooker, combine sausage, navy beans, carrots, celery, yellow onion, pepper, cumin, red pepper, bay leaf, and chicken broth.

Cook on low heat for 8 hours or until beans are tender.

Immediately before serving, stir in parsley. Garnish with crumbled bacon and green onions. Serve over rice.

Frenchmen Street Red Beans and Rice Soup

Steps away from the crowds of Bourbon Street, we locals like to enjoy the sights and sounds of the New Orleans music scene on Frenchmen Street. With venue after venue featuring the most eclectic musicians and a huge spectrum of musical genres, it is the perfect environment for appreciating the creative and artistic spirit so unique to our city.

This soup is a riff on one of the most traditional New Orleans dishes, red beans and rice. *Serves 6-8*

1 lb. dried red kidney beans
¾ cup of brown rice,
   uncooked
½ cup finely chopped red
   onion
2 links andouille sausage,
   sliced into ½" rounds

1 14.5-oz. can diced tomatoes
4 cups vegetable broth
6-8 cups water
1 tsp. cumin
1 tsp. black pepper
1 tsp. salt

Combine all ingredients in the slow cooker. Be sure to add enough water to leave 3" of space from the rim of the slow cooker, but no more than 8 cups.

Cook on low heat for 7 to 8 hours, until the beans and rice are tender.

Corn and Crab Bayou Bisque

If you make this soup for your family once, you surely will be making it again . . . and often. This soup is light enough to serve year round, and its mild flavor makes it the perfect opening act to any meal. To make it even more of a crowd favorite, we like to serve it in a fresh bread bowl. *Serves 4-6*

½ onion, chopped
1 cup chopped celery
¼ cup chopped green bell pepper
3 6-oz. jars marinated artichoke hearts, drained
½ cup butter, melted
2 15-oz. cans corn, drained
2 14.5-oz. cans chicken broth
2 cups milk

1 cup heavy whipping cream
4 slices American cheese
½ tsp. Worcestershire sauce
½ tsp. salt
½ tsp. pepper
½ tsp. garlic powder
½ tsp. parsley
Dash hot sauce
1 lb. fresh lump crab meat

On the stovetop, sauté onion, celery, bell pepper, and artichoke hearts in butter. Place in the slow cooker and add all other ingredients, except for crab meat.

Cook on high heat for 3 to 4 hours.

Around 20 to 30 minutes before serving, add the crab meat and heat through.

Flambeaux Gumbo

We are fortunate to have several talented gentlemen in the family who love to cook. When he's not wrangling grandkids, Papa Kononchek is in the kitchen whipping up new recipes.

Papa K's slow-cooker chicken and sausage gumbo is downright delicious. It is thick, hearty, perfectly seasoned, and you would never guess that it doesn't require the most labor-intensive step of most gumbos—making a roux. *Serves 4-6*

1 lb. andouille or smoked sausage, sliced into ½" rounds
1 lb. boneless, skinless chicken breast or thighs, cut into bite-sized pieces
10 oz. chopped okra, thawed if frozen
1 onion, chopped
3 stalks celery, chopped
1 bell pepper, chopped
2 garlic cloves, minced
1 14.5-oz. can petite diced tomatoes, undrained

1 14.5-oz. can chicken broth
1 tsp. thyme
2 bay leaves
½ tsp. salt
½ tsp. black pepper
½ tsp. onion powder
½ tsp. red pepper flakes
½ tsp. Kitchen Bouquet Browning & Seasoning Sauce
2 cups water

Add all ingredients to the slow cooker and stir.

Cook on low heat for 8 hours.

Serve over fluffy white rice.

Orleans Oyster and Artichoke Soup

Many of New Orleans's finest restaurants serve variations of this soup. Some use cream, and some do not. However, there is no denying that oysters and artichokes are a match made in . . . New Orleans! A Papa Keller original, this is our favorite version of this beloved soup. *Serves 4-6*

½ onion, chopped
½ cup chopped celery
2 6-oz. jars marinated
   artichoke hearts, drained
½ cup butter, melted
2 14.5-oz. cans chicken broth
2 cups milk
1 cup heavy whipping cream

½ tsp. salt
½ tsp. pepper
½ tsp. garlic powder
½ tsp. parsley
Dash hot sauce
3 dozen fresh oysters, drained
¼ cup chopped green onions

On the stovetop, sauté onion, celery, and artichoke hearts in butter.

Place in the slow cooker and add all other ingredients, except for oysters and green onions.

Cook on high heat for 3 to 4 hours.

Around 20 to 30 minutes before serving, add the oysters and green onions. When oysters start to curl around the edges, the soup is ready to serve.

Audubon Zoo Shrimp and Okra Stew

"I went on down to the Audubon Zoo,
and they all ask'd for you!"

It isn't hard to get this classic song's lyrics stuck in your head. Sing it while your slow cooker simmers away, creating this wholesome, satisfying dish with a kick. A great recipe for a seafood-only meal, it will have your guests all asking for the recipe. *Serves 6-8*

1 green bell pepper, chopped
1 onion, chopped
3 cloves garlic, minced
2 tbsp. butter
3 tbsp. lemon juice
¾ cup vegetable or chicken stock
1 14.5-oz. can diced tomatoes, undrained

1 10-oz. can diced tomatoes with chilies
2 tbsp. flour
1 tsp. Creole seasoning
1 lb. fresh shrimp
1 lb. chopped fresh okra

On the stovetop, sauté the bell pepper, onion, and garlic in butter until onions are translucent.

Place in the slow cooker and add all remaining ingredients, except for shrimp and okra. Cook on low heat for 6 to 8 hours.

Approximately 30 minutes before serving, add shrimp and okra. Cook until the shrimp are heated through and pink but not rubbery.

Serve over fluffy white rice.

Tchoupitoulas Chili

A bustling avenue for port commerce as well as commercial shops, Tchoupitoulas Street is home to restaurants, hotels, Hansen's snowball stand, and Tipitina's. Being able to pronounce the street's name is perhaps one of the truest tests of New Orleans culture, and we admittedly get a chuckle out of visitors' attempts at sounding it out.

We love this recipe on chilly, humid winter days. If you want to make a leaner version, it also tastes great using ground turkey meat. *Serves 6-8*

2 lbs. ground beef or ground chuck
1 white onion, chopped
4 garlic cloves, minced
1 15-oz. can red kidney beans
1 15-oz. can pinto beans
2 10-oz. cans diced tomatoes with chilies
1 15-oz. can tomato sauce

2½ tsp. chili powder
1 tsp. cumin
1 tsp. black pepper
½ tsp. salt
Sour cream, for topping
Shredded cheddar cheese, for topping
Corn or tortilla chips, for serving

Brown the meat on the stovetop.

Place the meat in the slow cooker and add all remaining ingredients except for sour cream, cheese, and chips. Stir.

Cook on low heat for 8 hours.

Top with a dollop of sour cream and shredded cheese. Serve with chips on the side for dipping.

Entrées

Royal Street Red Beans

The Creole dish of red beans and rice has been part of our cuisine for centuries. Traditionally, ham or pork was served on Sundays, and Monday was wash day. Because the beans could cook on the stove all day, it was the perfect meal to use the leftover ham and free up several hours away from the stove while tending to the laundry. You might even say this meal was one of our ancestors' original slow-cooker recipes! *Serves 6-8*

1 lb. dried red beans	3 bay leaves
1 white onion, diced	½ tsp. Creole seasoning
2 stalks celery, diced	½ tsp. Worcestershire sauce
4 garlic cloves, minced	6 cups water
1 lb. andouille or smoked sausage, thinly sliced	Green onions, for garnish
1 ham hock, optional	Hot sauce or seasoned vinegar to taste, if desired

Add all ingredients except for green onions and hot sauce to the slow cooker and stir.

Cook on low heat for 8 hours.

Before serving, remove bay leaves and garnish with green onions. Season with hot sauce or a splash of seasoned vinegar, if desired.

Serve over fluffy white rice.

Where Y'at? White Beans

The Yat dialect is specific to New Orleans, and we're proud of it. Phrases such as "where y'at?," "who dat," "makin' groceries," "ya mama 'n' 'dem," and po' boys—they're all part of our endearing vernacular.

Like our Royal Street Red Beans, these beans can sit in the slow cooker all day, and they just get better and better. The ham and sausage add a lot of depth to this dish and saturate the beans with flavor. *Serves 6-8*

3 tbsp. olive oil
1 lb. dried baby lima beans
1 lb. andouille sausage, cut in
 ½" slices
1 lb. ham, cubed
2 medium onions, chopped
2 stalks celery, chopped

4 green onion stalks, chopped
5 cups water
1 10-oz. can chicken broth
2 tsp. Creole seasoning
2 tsp. crab boil seasoning
½ tsp. sage
1 tsp. garlic powder

Add all ingredients to the slow cooker and stir.

Cover and cook on low heat for 8 hours or until beans are tender.

Serve over fluffy white rice.

Laissez les Bons Temps Rouler
Shrimp Étouffée

This traditional New Orleans dish lauds the mantra of our city: *Let the good times roll!* Translated "smothered" in French, a New Orleans étouffée is a delectable medley of vegetables, seasoning, and seafood. Allow your slow cooker to take care of creating the perfect étouffée, and laissez les bons temps rouler! *Serves 6-8*

2 tbsp. olive oil
2 tbsp. flour
1 tsp. Kitchen Bouquet Browning
   and Seasoning Sauce
2 cups diced onion
1 green bell pepper, diced
1 cup diced celery
¼ cup minced flat-leaf parsley
3 cloves garlic, minced
1 14.5-oz. can diced tomato

1 15-oz. can seafood stock
½ cup heavy whipping cream
1 tsp. Creole seasoning
½ tsp. black pepper
¼ tsp. cayenne pepper, or to
   taste
1 tsp. salt
2 bay leaves
2 lbs. fresh shrimp, peeled

Combine oil, flour, and Kitchen Bouquet in the slow cooker and stir until mixture is smooth.

Combine all other ingredients, except for shrimp, in the slow cooker and stir. Cook on high heat for 2 to 3 hours.

Approximately 30 to 45 minutes before serving, add shrimp, and cook until shrimp are pink and heated through but not rubbery.

Serve over fluffy white rice.

Jazzy Jambalaya

While most of us Louisianians love our jambalaya, few of us know the difference between Cajun and Creole Jambalaya. Creole Jambalaya is more common to the city of New Orleans. With a tomato base, it is a "red jambalaya." It also contains seafood and what we New Orleanians refer to as the trinity: onions, bell peppers, and celery. Cajun jambalaya is found more often in the rural bayous of Louisiana—check out our Jammin' Jambalaya recipe to see the difference! *Serves 6-8*

1 lb. smoked sausage, sliced
   into ½" rounds
1 white onion, chopped
2 stalks celery, diced
1 green bell pepper, diced
2 tsp. minced garlic
2 cups chicken broth
1 tsp. Creole seasoning

1 tsp. Worcestershire sauce
½ tsp. thyme
2 14.5-oz. cans diced tomato,
   undrained
¾ lb. jumbo shrimp, peeled
2 cups long-grain rice,
   cooked according to
   package directions

Combine all ingredients except for shrimp and rice in the slow cooker.

Cook on low heat for 7 to 8 hours.

Approximately 30 to 45 minutes before serving, add shrimp and cooked rice and stir. Cook until shrimp are pink and opaque but not rubbery.

Jammin' Jambalaya

Cajun Jambalaya hails from what we call "da bayou." It is also known as "brown jambalaya" (contrary to "red," or Creole jambalaya) and contains few vegetables. It often looks similar to dirty rice. Cajun jambalaya has a more complex, spicier flavor and more texture than the Creole jambalaya. We like to add the rice about half an hour before serving to avoid it getting too mushy. *Serves 6-8*

2 lbs. boneless, skinless chicken thighs, cut into pieces
1 lb. andouille sausage, sliced into ½" rounds
1 white onion, chopped
2 tsp. minced garlic

2 cups beef broth
1 tsp. Creole seasoning
1 tsp. Worcestershire sauce
½ tsp. thyme
2 cups long grain rice, cooked

Combine all ingredients, except for rice, in the slow cooker.

Cook on low heat for 7 to 8 hours.

Add cooked rice to slow cooker 30 minutes before serving and stir.

Rex Roast

Here in New Orleans, Rex reigns supreme as one of our oldest and most revered Mardi Gras krewes. Every year, we wait with anticipation for the Mayor to toast Rex, the King of Carnival, and officially commence the citywide revelry of Mardi Gras Day.

This roast is a classic pot roast with a New Orleans twist. Toss in some potatoes and carrots, and you'll have a meal fit for a king! *Serves 6-8*

1 5-lb. pot roast	2 10-oz. cans chicken broth
6-8 cloves garlic, peeled	1 packet onion soup mix
½ tsp. salt	2 cups water
½ tsp. pepper	4-5 new potatoes, chopped
½ tsp. Creole seasoning	5 carrots, chopped

Cut 6 to 8 slits in the roast and insert whole cloves of garlic. Sprinke salt, pepper and creole seasoning over the roast. Place roast in the slow cooker.

In a separate bowl, combine broth, onion soup mix, and water. Mix well. Slowly pour the liquid over the roast.

Cook on low heat for 8 hours.

Add potatoes and carrots 1 to 2 hours before serving.

Gris Gris Grits and Grillades

Our city is mostly perceived as a lively, upbeat, colorful town, full of celebration and fanfare. However, New Orleans has a darker, more mystical side, full of folklore, unsolved mysteries, haunted houses, cemetery tours, voodoo priestesses, and superstitions.

While very few of us dabble in voodoo, it is common knowledge that to put a "gris gris" on someone is to put a spell on them. Pile this delicious, tender meat on top of some warm, buttery grits and watch your guests fall under the spell of this dish! *Serves 6*

6 veal cutlets, thinly pounded
1 tbsp. Creole seasoning
½ cup butter
1 onion, chopped
1 8-oz. can diced tomatoes
1 8-oz. can tomato sauce
2 cups beef stock

1 cup water
1½ tbsp. Worcestershire sauce
Salt and pepper to taste
Grits with butter, for serving, prepared according to package

Rub down the veal with Creole seasoning and slightly brown in skillet on stovetop. Place veal in the slow cooker.

Add all remaining ingredients to slow cooker.

Cook on low heat for 8 hours.

Serve over grits with butter.

Decatur Daube

Architecture, cuisine, customs, arts, street names—it seems that every facet of New Orleans has been touched by French influence. On Decatur Street, between the French Market and Café du Monde, stands a gilded statue of Joan of Arc, gifted to the city by the people of France. Along with another Decatur Street-statue of New Orleans's founder, Jean-Baptiste Le Moyne, Sieur de Bienville, she is a tangible reminder of our inextricable cultural ties.

This dish pays homage to our French heritage. *Serves 6-8*

1 2-lb. chuck roast
1 medium yellow onion,
    chopped
2 cloves garlic, minced
¼ cup red wine
1 14.5-oz. can beef broth
2 12-oz. can tomato paste

2 tbsp. sugar
1 tsp. black pepper
2 sprigs fresh thyme
1 sprig fresh rosemary
Cooked egg noodles, for
    serving

Place all ingredients, except for noodles, in the slow cooker.

Cook on low heat for 6 to 8 hours.

Serve over cooked egg noodles.

Baronne Street Bruscialoni

This dish can be found on Italian restaurant menus across the New Orleans metropolitan area from Chalmette to Mid-City to the Northshore. Although the fillings—and even the spellings—differ from menu to menu, the appeal is universal.

This version, created by Patrice's husband, Chris, certainly possesses a "wow factor" both in taste and in presentation. When you slice into the tender meat to reveal the colorful spiral within, no one will believe that this was made in a slow cooker! *Serves 4-6*

2 1-lb. top round steaks
2 tsp. olive oil
2 cloves garlic, minced
½ cup Italian bread crumbs
½ lb. prosciutto
½ cup parmesan-Romano
 blend cheese

2 hard-boiled eggs, sliced
2 14-oz. jars pasta sauce
2 cups water, plus additional if
 needed

Lightly flatten the meat and rub the top side with olive oil and garlic.

Evenly layer bread crumbs, prosciutto, cheese, and egg slices on top of the seasoned meat.

Roll up meat carefully and secure with twine, using approximately 4 evenly spaced loops around each roll of meat. Place the two secured rolls of meat in the slow cooker.

Add pasta sauce to the slow cooker, then add water, being sure to just cover the meat.

Cook on low heat for 5 to 6 hours or until meat is tender.

Muffuletta Mambo Pasta

The muffuletta sandwich is a trophy of our city's cuisine. Created by Sicilian immigrants, it consists of various meats and cheeses on a large, toasted, sesame seed-sprinkled bun. But we New Orleanians know that the special ingredient is the olive salad.

As an ode to our favorite sandwich, we used many of the same ingredients to create a slow-cooker-friendly pasta dish that mirrors the flavors of the famous muffuletta. Serve with hot sesame-topped Italian bread on the side to complete the experience! *Serves 6-8*

3 boneless, skinless chicken breasts
1 tsp. salt
⅓ tsp. pepper
4 cloves garlic, minced
1 tsp. dried Italian seasoning
½ onion, chopped
¼ cup chopped green bell pepper
4 tbsp. olive oil
1 cup sliced mushrooms, canned or fresh
3 tbsp. capers
1 24-oz. jar pasta sauce
2 oz. pepperoni, sliced
Cooked pasta, preferably angel hair, for serving
1 cup olive salad
1½ cups shredded mozzarella cheese

Cube chicken breasts and place on the bottom of the slow cooker. Sprinkle chicken with salt, pepper, garlic, and Italian seasoning. Top chicken with onion, bell pepper, olive oil, mushrooms, and capers.

Pour pasta sauce over vegetables and top with pepperoni slices.

Cook on low heat for 6 hours.

When finished cooking, stir well. Serve over cooked pasta. Top with olive salad and mozzarella cheese.

Mid-City Meatballs

With its small restaurants and quaint bars nestled within the neighborhood streets, Mid-City is one of our favorite parts of town. Among our top places to visit are the hole-in-the-wall Italian restaurants and the famed Angelo Brocato's ice cream parlor and Italian pastry shop.

When we can't get away to our favorite local haunts, this hearty and satisfying meal fits the bill. *Serves 6-8*

½ lb. ground chuck
½ lb. ground veal
½ lb. ground pork
2 eggs
1 tsp. salt
3 garlic cloves, minced
⅓ onion, diced
1 cup parmesan cheese
½ cup Italian breadcrumbs
1 tbsp. sweet basil

1 tsp. oregano
1 tsp. parsley
1 28-oz. can peeled San Marzano tomatoes
1 14-oz. jar meat-flavored pasta sauce
1 5-oz. can tomato sauce with Italian herbs
½ cup water

In a large bowl, mix all ingredients except for tomatoes, pasta sauce, tomato sauce, and water. With your hands, form the mixture into balls with a 2" diameter.

Place the meatballs in the slow cooker and cover with tomatoes, pasta sauce, tomato sauce, and water.

Cook on low heat for 8 hours until cooked through.

Irish Channel Corned Beef and Cabbage

In the melting pot of New Orleans culture, our Irish heritage is one of the lesser-known components. However, the Irish played a pivotal role in the history and development of this great city. Lauren's ancestors' landing here can be traced to the year 1825.

Today, many Irish pubs are scattered around town, and we refer to the area where many immigrants settled as the Irish Channel. Every year, in addition to attending local St. Patrick's Day parades and festivities, we like to celebrate the Irish by making this recipe. *Serves 6-8*

3 pounds corned beef
1 onion, chopped
1½ cups water
1 14-oz. can chicken broth

4 carrots, chopped
1 head cabbage, broken apart

Rinse the corned beef and cut off excess fat.

Place the onion on the bottom of the slow cooker.

Place the corned beef on top of the onion.

Add water, chicken broth, carrots and cabbage.

Cook on low heat for 8 to 10 hours, or until meat is cooked and vegetables are tender.

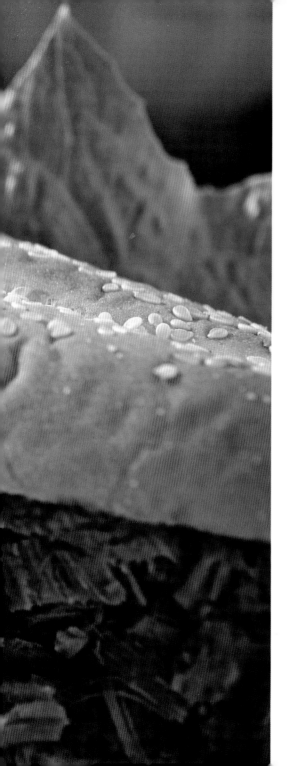

French Quarter French Dip

This is our version of the classic French Dip sandwich. It is similar to a New Orleans roast beef po' boy with a dynamite sauce on the side. We like to use French bread and a full-flavored beer from a local brewery. Provide each person with their own bowl of au jus sauce for dipping, and tuck in to a messy but delicious feast! *Serves 6-8*

4 lb. rump roast
6-8 cloves garlic
Salt and pepper to taste
1 14.5-oz. can beef broth
1 12-oz. beer
1 10.5-oz. can condensed
  French onion soup

1 tsp. Worcestershire sauce
French bread, for serving
Mayonnaise, for serving
Swiss cheese, for serving
Sliced red onions, for serving

Trim excess fat from the rump roast. Cut evenly spaced small slits in the sides of the roast and insert garlic cloves.

Place roast in the slow cooker and sprinkle with salt and pepper.

Around the sides of the roast, pour in beef broth, beer, condensed soup, and Worcestershire sauce.

Cook on low heat for 6 to 8 hours, or until meat is cooked and tender.

Cut roast into thin slices and serve on French bread dressed with mayonnaise, cheese, and red onions.

Use the gravy as dipping sauce.

Crabby Chicken

Papa Keller is one of those cooks who can turn a few random ingredients into a meal fit for the ages. For this recipe, he wanted to liven up some chicken breasts, and he saw that he had some crab boil seasoning on hand. The unlikely combination resulted in what is now one of our family's favorite recipes.

Use this chicken to make the best chicken salad you'll ever taste, and make it a meal with a light coleslaw. *Serves 4-6*

2 onions, chopped
½ cup celery, chopped
4 bone-in chicken breasts
1 tsp. salt

1 tsp. pepper
1 tsp. Creole seasoning
2 tbsp. crab boil seasoning
Water

Place onions and celery in the slow cooker.

Place chicken on top of the vegetables and sprinkle with salt, pepper, and Creole seasoning.

Add enough water to the slow cooker to reach 3-4" from the rim. Add crab boil seasoning to the water.

Cook on low heat for 5 to 6 hours.

_____

Crabby Chicken Salad

Serves 4-6

1 recipe crabby chicken,
   deboned and shredded
1 stalk celery, finely chopped

¼ cup chopped green onion
Hard-boiled eggs, chopped,
   optional

Combine all ingredients and serve chilled on croissants with coleslaw.

_____

Coleslaw

2 cups shredded cabbage,
   washed and dried
¼ cup mayonnaise, or to taste
½ tsp. garlic salt

2 tbsp. extra virgin olive oil
1 tbsp. vinegar
Salt and pepper to taste

Place all ingredients in a large bowl and stir well.

St. Charles Avenue Chicken and Dumplings

In New Orleans, there is nothing more picturesque than the scene of a dark green streetcar making its way down oak tree-lined St. Charles Avenue. As it clacks past parks, churches, universities, and historic mansions, it evokes a sense of nostalgia from pedestrians and passengers alike.

This Southern recipe is reminiscent of simpler times. It is perfect for a quiet evening at home with your loved ones. *Serves 6-8*

1½ lbs. boneless, skinless
   chicken thighs or breasts,
   cut into 1" cubes
2 cups chopped carrots
1 medium onion, diced
2 stalks celery, chopped
1 10¾-oz. can condensed
   cream of chicken soup

1 10¾-oz. can condensed
   cream of celery soup
1½ cups chicken broth
1 tsp. thyme
¼ tsp. pepper
1 6-oz. can refrigerated
   biscuits, cut into bite size
   pieces

Place chicken, carrots, onion, and celery in the slow cooker.

In a separate bowl, combine chicken soup, celery soup, chicken broth, thyme, and pepper. Mix well. Pour soup mixture over chicken and vegetables.

Cook on low heat for 7 to 8 hours.

Raise heat to high 30 to 45 minutes before serving, and add biscuit pieces. Cook until dough is cooked in the center.

Pontalba Pork Chops

Flanking Jackson Square are the iconic twin Pontalba buildings. For more than a century, the view from their wrought-iron balconies has not changed all that much. One can still see the horse-drawn carriages lining Decatur Street, the steamboats churning through the waters of the Mississippi, and the street performers and artists gathered in front of St. Louis Cathedral.

This recipe, a favorite of Lauren's husband, Rob, makes it effortless to create a classic, timeless meal. *Serves 4*

1 14-oz. bag herb-seasoned stuffing
4 boneless pork chops

2 cups chicken broth
¼ cup butter, cubed

Grease the slow cooker.

Spread a thin layer of stuffing along the bottom of the slow cooker.

Place two pork chops side by side on top of stuffing.

Add another layer of stuffing, then add remaining pork chops.

Top with remaining stuffing.

Evenly pour the chicken broth over the top layer of stuffing and top with cubes of butter.

Cook on low heat for 3 to 4 hours or until stuffing forms a crust and the center of the meat turns white.

Mais Oui Cochon de Lait

In French, *cochon de lait* means "suckling pig." In Cajun country, cochon de lait is made by marinating and then slow roasting suckling pigs on a spit.

Making true cochon de lait at home on a weeknight is not exactly practical. This recipe, however, provides fantastic, flavorful slow-cooked meat so tender that it falls apart. One of our favorite ways to eat it is on French bread as a po' boy. *Serves 4-6*

1 4-5-lb. pork butt
6 cloves garlic, whole
1 tsp. Dijon mustard
1 tbsp. chili powder

1 tbsp. black pepper
1 tsp. coriander
1 12-oz. can beer
1 12-oz. can beef broth

Cut 6 evenly spaced slits in top of pork butt and insert a garlic clove into each slit. Place pork butt in the slow cooker.

Spread mustard over the top of the meat.

In a separate bowl, combine chili powder, pepper, and coriander. Sprinkle spice mixture evenly over the top of the meat.

Pour beer around the pork, not over the top. Add enough beef broth to bring the liquid near the top of the pork, but do not cover.

Cook on low heat for 6 to 8 hours or until pork falls apart.

Magazine Street Mirlitons

Though mirlitons are a quirky vegetable seldom recognized outside our region, they are a staple in our cooking.

The most challenging part of using mirlitons in dishes is the need to watch the stovetop for hours as they boil until tender. We finish our stuffed mirlitons in the oven, but we take a shortcut by enlisting the slow cooker to do the prep work. *Serves 4*

4 mirlitons, whole
1½ cups chopped onions
4 stalks celery, chopped
1 cup chopped green onions
2 lbs. fresh shrimp, peeled,
**   deveined, and chopped**

½ cup butter
1½ cups Italian breadcrumbs
Salt and pepper to taste

Place mirlitons in the slow cooker and fill the slow cooker three-quarters full with water.

Cook on high heat for 3 to 4 hours, until mirlitons are tender.

Remove the mirlitons and cut in half. Scoop out the meat, leaving the shells as intact as possible, and set the shells aside.

Sauté the mirliton meat along with onions, celery, green onions, and shrimp in butter on the stovetop.

Remove from heat and mix with breadcrumbs.

Fill mirliton shells with the mixture and bake in a 350-degree oven for 30 to 40 minutes.

Sides

Calliope Corn Grits

Not many chain restaurants find success here in New Orleans . . . unless, of course, it's a chain that originated here. Zea's Rotisserie and Grill is one such exception.

Inspired by our favorite Zea's side dish, roasted corn grits, it took a lot of experimenting to create a version that worked for the slow cooker. We think that you'll be pleased with the result! *Serves 6-8*

1 cup yellow stone-ground grits
1 pt. heavy whipping cream
1 14.5-oz. can chicken broth

1 15-oz. can corn, drained
¼ cup butter, melted
1 tsp. kosher salt
¼ tsp. black pepper

Find a heat-proof bowl at least 1½ qt. in size that fits inside the slow cooker.

Combine all ingredients in the bowl and stir. Place bowl in the slow cooker.

In the slow cooker, pour water around the base of the bowl until bowl is two-thirds submerged.

Cook on low heat for 6 to 8 hours or until creamy.

City Park Corn Bread

Because New Orleans is surrounded by water, the land is tightly developed. However, in the middle of the urban sprawl lies our oasis of City Park: thirteen hundred acres of ancient oaks, lagoons, a botanical garden, an amusement park, an art museum, horse stables, tennis courts, and a golf course. The next time that you spend a day at the park, pack a picnic and include a few pieces of this delicious, zesty Southern corn bread. *Serves 6-8*

2 cups corn meal
½ cup all-purpose flour
1 tsp. baking powder
½ tsp. baking soda
½ tsp. salt

1 tsp. sugar
1 egg
1 cup buttermilk
1 15-oz. can creamed corn
1 4-oz. can diced chilies

Grease the slow cooker.

In a separate bowl, mix together corn meal, flour, baking powder, baking soda, salt, and sugar.

Add egg, buttermilk, creamed corn, and chilies, and blend well.

Spread mixture evenly in the slow cooker.

Cook on high heat for 3 to 4 hours or until a toothpick inserted in the center comes out clean.

Big Chief Corn Maque Choux

Whether it be Mardi Gras Day or Super Sunday (the Sunday closest to St. Joseph's Day), you know that percussion and a rainbow of feathers floating above the crowd means that the Mardi Gras Indians are marching your way. If you're lucky, you'll witness the procession of multiple tribes and a meeting of Big Chiefs clad in their vibrant, ornate costumes.

Like the Mardi Gras Indians, this corn maque choux (pronounced "mock shoe") is bold, colorful, and livens things up! *Serves 4-6*

2 cups corn niblets, thawed if frozen
2 tbsp. butter
1 cup onion, diced
1 green onion, chopped
½ cup chopped red bell pepper

1 clove garlic, chopped
½ cup heavy whipping cream
Dash hot sauce
Salt and pepper to taste

Grease the slow cooker.

Combine all ingredients in the slow cooker.

Cook on high heat for 1 to 2 hours, stirring occasionally, until corn is heated through and the sauce has thickened.

Garden District Green Beans

It's always fun to play tourist in your own city, to take a break from daily routine by hopping on a streetcar and moseying down St. Charles Avenue to the Garden District. You can spend a morning walking amid the spectacular architecture, the ornate, wrought-iron fences, and the stately oak trees. With a perceptive eye, you might be able to differentiate which houses were the original mansions with sprawling gardens and which were added later when lots were subdivided.

Use this recipe to liven up an ordinarily plain side dish and put some flavor into your dinner routine. *Serves 4-6*

2 cups whole green beans
1 small onion, chopped
½ cup chicken broth
Sea salt and freshly ground
    pepper to taste

6-8 slices bacon, cooked and
    crumbled

Place all ingredients, except for bacon, in the slow cooker.

Cook on low heat for 4 to 6 hours or high heat for 2 to 3 hours, until broth has mostly evaporated and beans are heated through and tender.

Before serving, sprinkle with crumbled bacon.

Canal Street Carrots

Canal Street winds from the river through downtown and Mid-City to become Canal Boulevard, where it stops at the lake. From hotels and high-rises, streetcars and oak trees, cemeteries and mansions, Canal Street is a slice of New Orleans culture. It links industry and commerce with leisure and whimsy.

Like Canal Street, this side dish ties everything together. Effortless to make, it is the perfect, sweet complement to any rich, savory New Orleans entrée. *Serves 6-8*

4 cups baby carrots   ¼ **tsp. salt**
1 cup brown sugar, packed   ½ **cup butter**

Combine all ingredients in the slow cooker.

Cook on low heat for 5 to 6 hours until carrots are tender.

Shotgun Sweet Potatoes

Shotgun homes, one of the primary architectural styles of New Orleans, showcase the charm and unparalleled craftsmanship of generations past. However, for those of us who have lived in a shotgun, we know the one main drawback: with no hallways, visitors must first tread through the living room and bedrooms to get to the kitchen, which is almost always located in the rear of the house.

A favorite at Thanksgiving, this delicious recipe affords you more time to clean your bedroom before the guests arrive! *Serves 6-8*

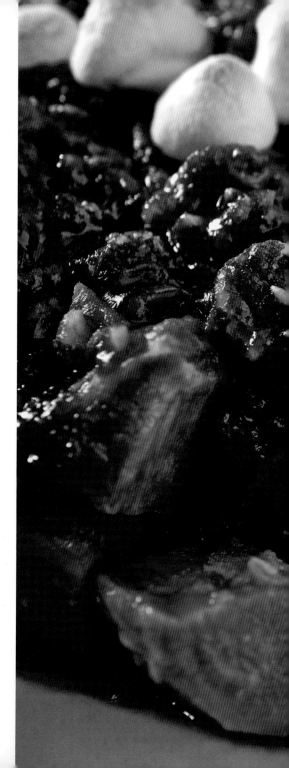

4 lbs. sweet potatoes, peeled and cubed
½ cup butter, softened, plus ¼ cup butter, melted, divided
1 cup white sugar
1 egg
2 tsp. vanilla extract
¼ tsp. salt
4 tbsp. flour, divided
½ cup pecans, chopped
½ cup dark brown sugar, packed
Mini-marshmallows, for topping, optional

Grease the slow cooker.

Place sweet potatoes in the slow cooker.

In a separate bowl, combine ½ cup butter, white sugar, egg, vanilla, salt, and 2 tbsp. flour. Blend mixture into the sweet potatoes.

In a separate bowl, combine remaining ¼ cup butter, brown sugar, pecans, and remaining 2 tbsp. flour. Sprinkle over the sweet potatoes.

Cook on low heat for 3 to 4 hours, until potatoes are tender.

If desired, sprinkle mini-marshmallows on top of the potatoes and cook for an additional 15 minutes before serving.

Prytania Potatoes

Among our favorite streets in the city, Prytania Street is home to beautiful Uptown residences, diverse restaurants, and the oldest movie theater in New Orleans, the Prytania Theatre, which opened in 1915.

Like Prytania Street, these potatoes are an old favorite. They are a simple, rustic side dish that pairs well with any entrée. *Serves 6-8*

3 lbs. red new potatoes, rinsed and quartered
2 tbsp. rosemary
2 tsp. rubbed sage
1 tsp. thyme
2 tsp. minced parsley

1 clove garlic, minced
2 tbsp. olive oil
½ cup butter, melted
¼ tsp. salt
½ tsp. ground pepper

Grease the slow cooker.

Add all ingredients to the slow cooker and stir gently.

Cook on high heat for 3 to 4 hours or until potatoes are tender.

Marconi Macaroni

From Mid-City to the lake, Marconi Drive is the scenic route. With a levee on one side and the edge of City Park on the other, it is a long, calming stretch of green. Rows of cypress trees grow alongside City Park's lagoon and fishing pier, and wildflowers blanket the grass in the spring. It is a perfect picture of quiet Southern living in the midst of a major city.

This recipe is the ultimate Southern comfort food, and it is always a hit with both adults and children. *Serves 8-10*

1 lb. sausage, cooked and chopped
½ lb. uncooked elbow pasta
3 cups milk
1 egg
2 tbsp. butter
1 14.5-oz can diced tomato, drained

½ tsp. salt
½ tsp. pepper
½ tsp. Creole seasoning
½ tsp. garlic powder
1 8-oz. block sharp cheddar cheese, shredded, divided

Grease the slow cooker.

In the slow cooker, add all ingredients except for half of the cheddar cheese.

Cook on high heat for 1½ to 2 hours, stirring occasionally, until pasta is cooked through.

Before serving, sprinkle the remaining shredded cheese on top of the macaroni.

Desserts

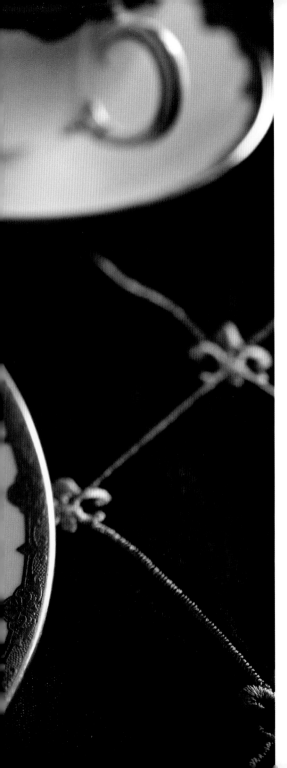

Broadway Bread Pudding

Decades ago, a small corner grocery store belonging to Lauren's great-grandparents sat Uptown on Broadway Street. Like many neighborhood stores of days past, the family lived upstairs and managed the grocery below.

A great way to salvage French bread that has sat on the shelf until just past its prime, this classic New Orleans dessert aims to please. *Serves 6-8*

For the Bread Pudding:
6 cups French bread, cut into 1" cubes
5 eggs
1 cup brown sugar
1 tsp. cinnamon
1 tsp. nutmeg
¼ tsp. salt
¼ cup butter, melted
2 cups heavy whipping cream
2 tsp. vanilla extract
2 tbsp. rum

For the Sauce:
½ cup butter
1 cup brown sugar, packed
¼ cup rum
3 tbsp. water
½ tsp. nutmeg
⅛ tsp. salt

For the Bread Pudding:

Grease the slow cooker.

Place bread pieces in the slow cooker.

In a separate bowl, beat the eggs; whisk in the brown sugar, cinnamon, nutmeg, salt, butter, cream, vanilla, and rum. Pour mixture over the bread; do not stir. With the back of a spoon, press down on bread so it absorbs the liquid.

Cook on high heat for 2 to 3 hours, or until a knife inserted in the center of the pudding comes out clean.

Note: If the bread is very stale, allow a few minutes for the liquid to be absorbed before turning on slow cooker.

For the Sauce:

On the stovetop, melt the butter in small saucepan over medium heat.

Add remaining ingredients. Stir constantly until sugar is dissolved and desired consistency is reached.

Drizzle over plated bread pudding.

White Linen Bread Pudding

In August, at the peak of New Orleans heat and humidity, we head down to the Warehouse District for White Linen Night. Joining thousands decked out in white linen attire (and the occasional seersucker suit), we hop from art gallery to art gallery along Julia Street and take in the sights, sounds, and cuisine of the Arts District celebration.

This decadent white chocolate bread pudding is a twist on traditional New Orleans bread pudding. It is very rich on its own, but feel free to top with a caramel sauce for extra sweetness. *Serves 6-8*

6 cups French bread, cut into 1" cubes
1½ cups white chocolate chips, divided
7 large egg whites
½ cup half-and-half
2 cups milk
1 14-oz. can sweetened condensed milk
¾ cup warm water
½ cup sugar
3 tbsp. butter, melted
1½ tsp. vanilla extract
½ tsp. cinnamon

Grease the slow cooker.

Place bread in the slow cooker. Top with half of the white chocolate chips.

In a separate bowl, combine egg whites, half-and-half, both milks, water, sugar, butter, vanilla, and cinnamon. Pour mixture over white chocolate chips in the slow cooker. With the back of a spoon, press down on the bread so it absorbs the liquid.

Spread remaining white chocolate chips on top of bread mixture.

Cook on low heat for 3 to 4 hours, or until a knife inserted in the center of the pudding comes out clean.

Picayune Pecan Pie

First published as the *Picayune* in 1837, the *New Orleans Times-Picayune* has been the city's longstanding newspaper. It was originally the price of a picayune (a Spanish coin valuing roughly six cents), and its archives document our dear city's history, traditions, family records, and recipes, including several versions of this local favorite: pecan pie.

Louisiana's abundance of delicious pecans makes this a Thanksgiving tradition in many of our homes, including Nana Keller's. In fact, because Nana's birthday always falls around Thanksgiving, she requests this pie every year in place of a birthday cake!

Preparing this classic Southern dessert in the slow cooker will free up more oven space for a large turkey or turducken, another local favorite. *Serves 4-6*

1 pre-made refrigerated pie crust
3 eggs
⅔ cup corn syrup
6 tbsp. butter, melted

1 cup white sugar
¼ cup brown sugar
1 tsp. vanilla extract
2 tbsp. corn starch
1½ cups pecan halves

Grease the slow cooker.

Place the pie crust on the bottom of the slow cooker. The edge of the crust should curve up the sides of the slow cooker.

In a separate bowl, combine all remaining ingredients. Spread the mixture inside the pie crust.

Cook on high heat for 2 to 3 hours or until crust starts to brown.

Serve warm with vanilla ice cream.

Pontchartrain Candied Pecans

The New Orleans lakefront holds a special place in the hearts of locals. Residents from all parts of our city enjoy taking a ride out to Lakeshore Drive to relax, clear their minds, and watch the sailboats glide along Lake Pontchartrain. At any given time, one can see families eating crawfish, fishing along the sea wall, feeding the seagulls, riding bikes, or flying kites on top of the levee. Outings to the lakefront with their mother are among Lauren and her two sisters' favorite childhood memories.

   This is a simple recipe that is great to pack as a snack for a picnic; to bag up as small Christmas gifts for friends, teachers, and neighbors; or simply to use as a topping for a big bowl of your favorite ice cream. *Serves 6-8*

½ cup butter, melted
2 cups pecan halves
½ cup powdered sugar
1 tsp. vanilla extract

2 tsp. cinnamon
Pinch of ground ginger
Pinch of nutmeg
Pinch of cloves

Place melted butter in the bottom of the slow cooker.

Add all remaining ingredients and mix thoroughly.

Cook, uncovered, for 1½ hours on high heat, stirring every half hour.

Vieux Carré Chex Mix

More commonly known as the French Quarter, the Vieux Carré is the heart of our city. Full of history and tradition, it is where our ancestors settled after arriving in New Orleans centuries ago, and it remains the epicenter of our culture.

These recipes are near and dear to Patrice's family. Every year, Mama Jacobsen would make these slow-cooker adaptations of a well-known classic to kick off the holiday season. To the children of the family, these recipes mean Christmas. They are also great for sleepovers, football games, and Mardi Gras parties. We are including the recipes for our two favorite versions: one sweet, one savory. *Serves 8-10*

2-3 cups Rice Chex® cereal
2-3 cups Wheat Chex® cereal
1 cup popped popcorn
¾ cup butter, melted

Either:
1 cup pecans
2 cups powdered sugar
1 cup chocolate chips, melted
¼ tsp. vanilla extract

Or:
1 cup peanuts
2 cups unsalted pretzels
1 tsp. onion powder
1 tbsp. seasoned salt
Dash cayenne pepper
2 tbsp. Worcestershire sauce

Add rice cereal, wheat cereal, and popcorn to the slow cooker, along with *either* pecans and powdered sugar *or* peanuts, pretzels, onion powder, seasoned salt, and cayenne.

In a separate bowl, combine butter and *either* melted chocolate chips and vanilla extract *or* Worcestershire sauce.

Pour liquid mixture into slow cooker and stir carefully to combine well.

Cook, uncovered, for 1½ hours on low heat, stirring every half hour.

Serve in the slow cooker to keep the mix warm.

Big Easy Bananas Foster

Since 1946, the Brennan family has played a significant role in the restaurant scene of New Orleans. Today, various family members own more than a dozen esteemed restaurants, and we locals love to debate which reigns supreme on the Brennan hierarchy.

While not nearly as exciting as the fiery tableside presentation you'd experience at the original Brennan's restaurant, this slow-cooker version of bananas foster captures the flavor and essence of the dish. Just don't forget the vanilla ice cream! *Serves 6-8*

½ **cup butter, melted**
1 **cup brown sugar**
8 **bananas, cut lengthwise into**
   ½"-thick strips

¼ **cup rum**
½ **tsp. cinnamon**
Vanilla ice cream, for serving

Grease the slow cooker.

Place bananas in the slow cooker.

In a separate bowl, combine all other ingredients except for ice cream. Pour mixture over bananas.

Cook on low heat for 1 to 2 hours until banana slices are wilted and have absorbed flavor from the sauce.

Serve on top of vanilla ice cream.

Bienville Blueberry Cobbler

A favorite summer pastime for families in the area is heading to a Louisiana blueberry farm and gathering buckets and buckets of berries. With enough self-control, there will be enough to freeze to last until next season! There should also be enough to make a delicious batch or two of this beloved Southern dessert, blueberry cobbler.

This cobbler is light, fluffy, and the perfect summer treat. Best served warm and à la mode. *Serves 6-8*

4 cups blueberries, fresh or frozen
¾ cup plus 1 tbsp. white sugar, divided
¼ cup lemon juice

2 tbsp. cornstarch
2 cups baking mix
½ cup butter, melted
¾ cup milk

Grease the slow cooker.

Place blueberries, ¼ cup sugar, lemon juice, and cornstarch in the slow cooker. Gently stir to combine.

In a separate bowl, combine baking mix, ½ cup sugar, butter, and milk. Pour mixture on top of blueberry mixture.

Sprinkle the remaining 1 tbsp. sugar over the top.

Cook on high heat for 3 hours or until center of cobbler is slightly firm.

Mr. Bingle Cherry Delight

It's hard to think of a New Orleans Christmas without nostalgia for years past. We think of when it snowed on Christmas Day 2004. We think of our first Christmas back in our homes following Hurricane Katrina. We think of visiting the beautiful displays at hotels and in City Park, giving our memories warmth and holiday cheer. For decades, the mounting of the large papier-mâché Mr. Bingle outside Maison Blanche department store on Canal Street signaled the arrival of Christmas season in New Orleans. His ice cream cone hat, holly leaf wings, and cherry nose brought joy to children and adults alike.

This recipe will be sure to call all wonderful Christmases to mind. *Serves 6-8*

1 21-oz. can cherry pie filling	**1 box yellow cake mix**
1 20-oz. can crushed pineapple	**¾ cup butter, melted**
	1 cup pecans, finely chopped

Grease the slow cooker.

Place cherry filling on the bottom of the slow cooker. Add the crushed pineapple.

Evenly spread yellow cake mix over fruit.

Pour butter over the cake mix.

Sprinkle pecans on top.

Cook on high heat for 2 to 3 hours until center is set and edges begin to brown.

Note: Do not mix these ingredients! They are supposed to be in even layers.

Streetcar Strawberry Streusel

It comes as no surprise that the strawberry is the state fruit of Louisiana. For decades, hundreds of thousands of people of all ages have flocked to the annual Ponchatoula Strawberry Festival. We buy flats at a time of beautiful, bright red, sweet Louisiana strawberries.

We love to eat them plain, but when you want a quick and easy dessert, try this recipe. Use yellow cake mix and walnuts for a lighter flavor, or Devil's Food cake mix and chocolate chips for a treat that will satisfy the strongest of chocolate cravings. Serve warm on top of vanilla ice cream. *Serves 6-8*

1 pt. strawberries, sliced
1 tbsp. white sugar
1 tbsp. lemon juice
1 box yellow cake mix or
   Devil's Food cake mix

½ cup butter, softened
½ cup chopped walnuts or
   semi-sweet chocolate chips

Grease the slow cooker.

In a separate bowl, combine strawberries, sugar, and lemon juice. Spread strawberry mixture on the bottom of the slow cooker.

In a separate bowl, combine the butter and cake mix. Spread cake mixture over strawberries.

Top the cake mixture with walnuts or chocolate chips.

Cook for 1 to 2 hours on low heat, or until strawberry liquid begins to bubble up the sides of the slow cooker.

Serve on top of vanilla ice cream.

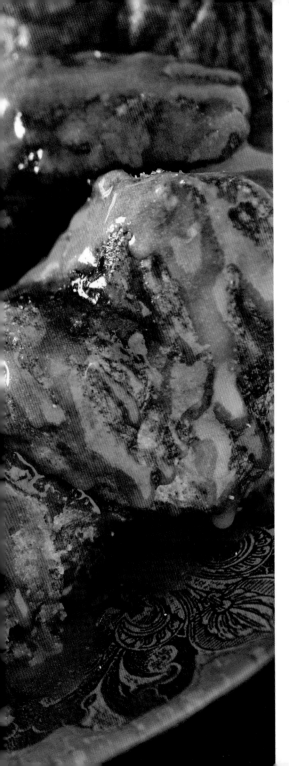

Twelfth Night King Cake

Twelfth Night not only marks the finale of the twelve days of Christmas but also the beginning of Carnival Season—and that means king cake.

We love to debate which bakery makes the best king cake (taste-testing is required). However, when you don't feel like waiting in line at your bakery of choice, or if you want to make king cake outside of Carnival season, this recipe, inspired by monkey bread, will do the trick! *Serves 6-8*

For the Cake:
1 16-oz. tube refrigerated
   jumbo-sized biscuits
½ cup butter, melted
1 cup white sugar
1 cup brown sugar, packed
1½ tbsp. cinnamon

For the Icing:
1 tbsp. milk
1 cup powdered sugar
1 tsp. vanilla extract
Food coloring, traditionally
   purple, green, and gold

For the Cake:

Grease the slow cooker.

Cut each biscuit into fourths and set aside.

Place the butter in a bowl.

In a separate bowl, combine sugar, brown sugar, and cinnamon.

Dip the biscuit pieces in butter, then dredge in the sugar mixture.

Arrange individual biscuit pieces in the slow cooker so that they are all touching, forming an oval around the perimeter.

Cook on high heat for approximately 2 hours or until dough is golden brown.

Note: Large, oval slow cookers work best for the most authentic-looking king cakes.

For the Icing:

In a large bowl, combine milk, powdered sugar, and vanilla extract. Divide into thirds and use food coloring to make purple, green, and gold icing.

Drizzle icing over cake, alternating colors.

Crescent City Crème Brûlée

Crème brûlée can be found in the finest of New Orleans restaurants.

Use your spoon to crack into this timeless New Orleans dessert's crisp sugary crust to reveal the rich, creamy custard below. *Serves 4*

5 egg yolks
2 cups heavy whipping cream
½ cup fine sugar

1 tsp. vanilla extract
¼ cup raw sugar, for the
    topping

Fit 4 heat-resistant ramekins inside the slow cooker. Fill the slow cooker with enough water to cover the bottom half of the ramekins. Remove ramekins from the slow cooker and set aside.

In a separate bowl, whisk egg yolks. While whisking, slowly add the cream, fine sugar, and vanilla extract. Pour mixture into ramekins and carefully place in the slow cooker.

Cover and cook on high heat for 2 to 3 hours or until custard is set.

Using oven mitts, remove ramekins from the slow cooker and let cool; once room temperature, chill them in refrigerator for 2 to 3 hours.

Sprinkle raw sugar across the top of each ramekin. Use a handheld cooking torch to melt and brown the sugar, creating a caramelized top.

Index